TABLE OF CONTENT

CHAPTER SIX   **FINANCIAL PROJECTION**

EXECUTIVE SUMMARY

CONSULTANTS FINDINGS, RECOMMENDATION AND CONCLUSION

CONSULTANTS FINDINGS

The proposed business project is the feasibility and market research for the product; Drone. A drone was initially referred to as an unmanned aerial vehicle (UAV). Going by its name, drone is just like an aircraft, which can be flown without the help of a human pilot as it's obtained in flying a normal planes and helicopters. Drone can be assumed as just a flying robot mechanism, which plays a great role in security by taking an aerial view of one's surround as well as environs as to ensure there is not security breach with regards to break in or illegal entry, film making, which saves the cost of flying an helicopter as to take an aerial view of a surrounding; this poses a threat to Nigerian film makers who cannot afford it but for the invention of drone, photography; drone now makes it easier to take pictures in an unsecured areas like crisis or war zone, which can't be penetrated by human beings like journalist and come out alive. All these also serve as the market for the product which is diversified.

Following our research, the project will cost an estimated sum of **N1, 870, 000** to take off. From survey and projections carried out, the labour capital provision for one month would be **N145, 000** while the operational expenses provision for six (6) months would be **N350, 000**. The enterprise is estimated to generate **N147, 160,000** naira annually

The proposed location for the project is best suited at Lagos state; one of the largest cities in Africa. In addition, a warehouse and stores will be acquired for the product business.

Lagos state was selected for this business because it will be more profitable if established there added to its large market, which is the biggest in Africa.

Lagos state alone has a population of about 20 million people (16 percent of Nigeria's population) the Largest in the country. Research findings shows that Lagos state has lots of rich individuals, businesses, companies as well as manufacturers capable of purchasing and using drone for their daily business and home use. Below are the advantages when established at it chosen location.

1. close to railway station 2minutes drive to the railway, which leads to the north & southern parts of Nigeria.
2. centered on the state urban market and about 55 minutes drive to Benin republic border with Nigeria.
3. close to the Murtala mohammed international airport; about 20 minutes drive

4. Close to lots of private and international corporate business offices and outlets for easy sales and delivery.
5. Surrounded by four states: ondo, ogun, ekiti and osun.
6. about 5 hours drive to Abuja; the state capital
7. Surrounded by ocean, seasonal and non-seasonal streams, which makes dispatch of products from port more easier.

Moreover, there is availability of electricity, good roads and experienced manpower in Lagos, which can hardly be obtained in other states of the country.

The product is targeted to be sold at the following local and international markets.

LOCAL MARKETS

Local markets are 36 states of Nigeria & Abuja; the state capital

INTERNATIONAL MARKETS

International markets are ECOWAS countries (Economic community of west African countries) and all other African countries.

Based on the financial projections of 40%, 50% and 60% in the 1st, 2nd and 3rd years respectively starting with average sales prediction. The projected revenue in the first year of operation will be **N147,160,000** this will increase from **N2,729,500** and **N4,922,300** based on 1st, 2nd, 3rd years respectively.

Gross profit would be **N150, 000,000, N300,000,000** and **N495,000,000** for 1ST, 2ND and 3RD year respectively with product price tagged 300,00 naira per one.

Operational expenses on the other hand for 1st, 2nd and 3rd year would be **N2, 295, 000, N2,160,000,** and **N2,225,000** respectively.

The projected cash flow statement is very promising with surplus cash flow of **N147, 705,000, N297, 840 and N492, 775** for 1st, 2nd and 3rd year respectively. The net profit can well be determined by you after the cost of product is deducted; an information, which is best known to you.

The fixed asset is **N1, 350,000** with cumulative depreciation of **375, 750,** and **1,125** which represents 1st, 2nd and 3rd year respectively

Based on the investment appraisal (viability and profitability test) carried out. The business is profitable and viable as well as easy to operate. Once it gets into Nigeria, the rest is story. Nigeria have the market and the human resources needed to afford the awesome invention due to its largely impact for the owner and the society in general. The business is also success-promising in the future why, because the market is yet untapped and should it started now prior to rise of competition the brand name must had being solidified against any backdrop. This is because businesses are now rated by their years of operation and quality services rendered, which is why no matter the challenges MTN might face; it will also stand out among the rest.

Views and recommendation

Based on the above finding from the research concluded, the following are recommended.

1   Procrastination must be avoided or else all numeration here will be altered. The rate of inflation in Nigeria today added to the unpredictable position the exchange rate has assumed in recent years implies the negative effect a delay can cause. Investment proposals are therefore prone to several and rapid cost escalation, if implementation is delayed.

2.   Though profits sponsoring jingles on televisions or radio is expensive as it will be done on national televisions (like Nigerian Television Authority (NTA), Silverbird Television, Channels Television and so many more as to first create a wide publicity at the start), the promoters are advised to embark on it since it will create a quicker awareness to consumers.

Conclusion

What we have done so far is a professional evaluation of the proposed business plan.

In the course of the study, all the viability and profitability tests carried out showed very impressive results.

In the absence of any legal, political, socio-economic or other restraint, the consultants are of the opinion that this project will contribute to the nations GNP, will also create employment opportunities for Nigerians, generate huge profits for the owners, add value to inputs and pay taxes and interest on the borrowed fund (if any).

Therefore, this project is seen as socially desirable, economically worthwhile, technically feasible, commercially viable and highly profitable.

Hence the consultants hereby do recommend this project for immediate acceptance and implementation.

PART ONE

INTRODCTION/PROJECT BACKGROUND

INTRODUCTION

Nigeria is the largest country in Africa with over a hundred and sixty million people. Meanwhile, it's obvious that despite the business growth challenges; with regards to security and cost of operation e.t.c indigenous private companies thrives due to Nigeria's big market, which is the largest in Africa, lack of tax payment, non implementation of social responsibility, and staff salary exploitation. To name but few.

The purpose of the project is to carry out a comprehensive feasibility studies on the successful sale of Drone (Tri-copter) product in Nigeria, Lagos to be specific in order to tap into the Nigerian market.

TERMS OF REFERENCE

The following terms of reference will observed in the course of the study:

i.   The research and report will carefully study the feasibility of the proposed project.

ii. Analysis of the cost and revenue implications of the operations, including cash flow, balance sheets and profits for the each of the first three years of operations

iii. A market study to determine the nature, characteristics and extent of the market for the proposed products, putting the strength, weaknesses, opportunities and threats surrounding the proposed project into consideration; and

iv. To determine the commercial viability and profitability of the proposed project.

OBJECTIVES OF THE STUDY

The overall objectives of this study are:

i. To provide the economic and financial implications or otherwise for this project.

ii. To examine the feasibility study and recommend the best technological option and operational modalities for the proposed investment.

iii. To determine the economic feasibility, commercial viability, financial logistics and profitability of establishing the project.

iv. To provide vital information for investment planning and execution.

SCOPE OF STUDY

This study will cover important aspects of the proposed projects such as

i. Market study, including the demand, supply, market size, targeted market, strategies and Prospects.

ii. Technical considerations such as plant specifications, machinery and equipment, production technology, raw materials requirements, fuel, oil, power and other such utilities. We will consider local sourcing of raw materials as well as production.

iii. Capital requirements for the project

iv. Manpower requirements, management and labor costs

v. Economic feasibility and financial analysis

vi. Commercial viability and profitability of the project

MEHODOLOGY

The data applied in this study were derived from verified information and recommendations based on findings and are highly reliable.

However, information and data were also sourced from the following institutions:-

i. Standard organization of Nigeria federal secretariat, Lagos.

ii. Federal office of statistics

iii. Some Nigerian top importers of likely product

iv. Open market research within Lagos and some major markets in the South-east and south-south geopolitical zones.

v. Associated or similar firms that are into sales of the product.

CHAPTER TWO

PROJECT BACKGROUND

BACKGROUND INFORMATION AND PROJECT CONCEPT

A drone was initially called an unmanned aerial vehicle (UAV). Going by its name, drone is just like an aircraft, which can be flown without the help of a human pilot as it's obtained in flying a normal planes and helicopters. Drone can be assumed as just a flying robot mechanism.

Drones are more used in situations where flights conducted by human beings are considered highly risky or unattainable. Good example is stronghold of terrorist group. Its obvious that no flight can make it out alive. In order not to risk lost of human lives as well as destruction of plane; drone was invented to serve as an alternative. Though, it was exclusively for the military but there has being an increasingly use of it for recreation and business. They are also referred to as unmanned aerial systems (UASs) by producers targeting civilian market.

Developmental history of drone is dated back to the un-manned, bomb-filled balloons deployed by Austria to attack Venice in 1849 war. The early 1900s witnessed increased interest in drone innovations and a number of remote-controlled aircraft were seen in the period around the First World War.

Today, drones are classified into two main types: autonomous aircraft and remotely-piloted aircraft. Autonomous UAVs are controlled by onboard computers, while the remotely-piloted variants are piloted with the use of a remote control from an outside location.

PROPOSED LOCATION OF THE PROJECT

The proposed location for the project is best suited at Lagos state; one of the largest cities in Africa. In addition, a warehouse and accommodation will be acquired for the product

Lagos state was selected for this business because it will be more profitable if established there added to its large market, which is the biggest in Africa.

Lagos state alone has a population of about 30 million people, the Largest in the country. Research findings shows that Lagos state has lots of rich individuals, businesses, companies as well as manufacturers capable of purchasing and using drone for their daily business and home use. Below are the advantages when established at it chosen location.

8. close to railway station 2mins drive, the railway leads to the north & southern parts of Nigeria
9. centered on the state urban market and about 35 minutes drive to Benin republic border with Nigeria
10. close to the Murtala mohammed international airport; about 20 minutes drive
11.

12. Close to lots of corporate business for easy sales and delivery
13. Surrounded by four states: ondo, ogun, ekiti and osun.
14. about 5 hours drive to Abuja; the state capital
15. Surrounded by ocean, seasonal and non-seasonal streams.

Moreover, there is availability of electricity, good roads and experienced manpower in Lagos, which can hardly be obtained in other states of the country.

LEGAL CONSIDERATION

Since drone is a product for Nigerian market, it must be first approved as well as attain the quality specified by Standard Organization of Nigeria (SON) and Nigeria Industrial Standard (NIS) and other relevant international agencies.

CERTIFICATION PROCEDURE

Following the import requirements of the federal republic of Nigeria, for an importer to import foreign product to Nigeria. It must obtain the following document.

(A) Product certificate (PC) Issued by Cotecna

(b) Certificate of Conformity (CoC), which is well known as SONCAP Certificate (SC), Issued by Cotecnac

Cotecna is authorized by Nigeria federal government to analyze any likely imported and exported products in Nigeria.

In a bid to curb the importation of fake goods into Nigeria, the federal government issued fresh guideline. On 1st of December 2013. Under the new directive, all documents must bear the product name, country of origin, specification, manufacturer, date and batch number, standards of production. For example, International Energy Standard (IES), International Organization for Standardization (ISO) and Documentation Identification Number (DIN). That's after the above certificates are obtained

FEES INVOLVED

Your level of import is graded on Route A Category; Product Certificate Unregistered or Unlicensed Product (UC), single model. The certificate is valid for six months at the cost of $300

SONCAP Certificate (SC) $300

Conformity Report $350 per shipment

The dollar is converted to naira at the calculation pages.

As a consultant we see this project as legally feasible. In addition, I believe the product has an official brand name.

ENVISAGED PROBLEMS AND PROSPECTS

Although, Nigeria has become the center for investors due to its huge population as well as market some challenges still poses a threat. Though, the market is large to accommodate all businesses, there are still lacks of infrastructure like electricity to support the businesses as well as reduce cost. Thousands of naira is to be spent in buying and fueling a stand by generator, which price must reflect on the product thereby increasing cost of operation as well as raising the price of product against the citizens. Another is insecurity; presently, Nigeria is a place where crime is on the increase; a store can be bugled over night added to all other forms of immorality. Good thing is that the product is for security purpose and will therefore play a great role in sales and protection, the harsh business environment; Nigerian business environment is rated harsh due to the instability of policies as well as unfavorable policies, which greatly kill businesses, lack of good roads and multiple taxation.

Stated above are some of the problems militating against the smooth operation of importing and selling of product in Nigeria.

THE PROSPECTS

Despite the problems militating against smooth operation of business in Nigeria, which can be presently summed as natural. It will never be a problem to the business specifically since its general. Rather it will save the business lots of cost why because not all the above problems will directly affect your level of business in

Nigeria. Especially on multiple taxation, electricity, roads and security, this is in regards to the business level.

CHAPTER THREE

ECONOMIC AND MARKET ANALYSIS

ECONOMIC REVIEW

By projection, Nigeria population is about 170 million people added to its large market, which is the largest in Africa. Nigeria's electronic and retail market has experienced great success. The boom in Nigeria's electronic and retail sector last year as stated by experts as well as both online and offline sales reports of big manufacturing and sales companies in Nigeria, is accorded to speedy economic development and favorable economic policies. Furthermore, the population of working class in Nigeria is increasing steadily with a disposable income. Lots of people are now able to purchase what they do buy outside no matter the price. All these made Nigeria the bride of investors. In fact the potential buying power of Nigerians inspired lots of investments by both local and foreign companies, which will also need the drone product for a better operation of their businesses. This should be the product target market.

Research shows that there are lots of individuals, private and public companies ready to buy the drone product for the surveillance and delivery of their products. The benefits of the product is many that lots of businesses and companies in Lagos, Abuja, Anambra, Kano, Kaduna and other states will need its services. The military is not left out here, which was the first focus of drone innovation prior to its impact on the civilian and commercial aspect.

The market for drone product in Nigeria is very large due to the security situation in the country. The security situation will make the demand for drone product to be very high in the future due to the awesome security role it plays. Compared to the financial and risk of hovering a human pilot helicopter over an area in surveillance, drone can be a great alternative at reduced cost and non-risk of human life. This implies that the drone market in Nigeria is yet untapped since many are yet to know or start using the product, which can be attributed to lack of awareness and enlightenment about the product. This is why advertisement resources must be reserved as to quickly boost the business. Nevertheless, since you are the producer, it might be awesome to produce it locally rather than import full developed products, which will also save cost and raise profit

It is the opinion of the federal government that establishment of those industries with some percent local inputs can generate employment for the masses, develop the local areas as well as lead to an increase in the country's gross domestic product .

The production or importation of drone products belongs to the category of products that can be produced using domestic resources, which is in line with the government industrial policies.

In addition, it is also of good intention to invest as well as contribute to the growth of the economy by investing in the country's market especially on the vital area of security; a worst present challenge facing the country..

MARKET ANALYSIS

The market for the product is majorly urban based. This is because the companies as well as rich individuals that can afford it are all based in the city. Is left for the buyer to send it to their respective grassroots homes for use or order its delivery. But the cities are the major point of sale for such price intensive product. It is fast expanding due to the steady search for security appliance and better secured standard of living among they citizens and instituted conglomerate business.

With regards to urban areas, the businesses are always in search of means of overcoming security challenges, which has resulted to unrealistic dead of lots of business policies in Nigeria. Not even staff of a company can be full trusted in security issues following lots of security breach by staff against its company. With the invention of drone, the bosses can be able to have a first hand of whatever that is going on in their environment without relying on human analyses, which can be twisted atimes. The tendency among the booming companies and individuals to heavily rely on accurate security view makes the business feasible. Because of these and the exploding population and businesses, the demand for drone product will continue to be on the increase.

Despite that the price of drone product is on the high side because of production cost and there is not enough supply to go round as well as competition to bring down the prices, which implies why the business will succeed.

THE SUPPLY POSITION OF DRONE PRODUCT

With regards to market survey carried out; here is one major distributor of the product while others deals in its parts, like cameras which are listed below as follows:

1. Gidi Drone Ltd

8b, Ogidi Crescent Off Admiralty Way,

Lekki phase 1,

Lagos, Nigeria

2.   Anchez Ventures

77, Aroloya street,

Lagos Island,

Lagos, Nigeria

3.   Sony Center

4b, Agoro Odiyan street,

Victoria insland,

Lagos, Nigeria

SALES (MARKETING) STRATEGY

The most important aspect of selling any product is marketing especially when the product is new in the market.

Therefore adequate sales plan must be mapped out before the product is introduced into the market.

Unfortunately, though, drone product is not yet a household name product in Nigeria so that makes the product much easier to sell once its good and well advertized.

People will buy any brand of the product once it has quality as well as serve the need of the customer.

As a new product, additional effort is always required to make the product penetrate the market. Theses may include:

1. Advertizing
2. Vigorous distribution
3. Credit facilities to the major distributors in the market

4.   Products can also be supplied shop to shop to retailers using marketing executives.

The most effective marketing strategy is to make the brand name popular by means of advertisement. This can only be achieved through media advert.

It should be noted that when consumers knows a particular product by name, the will always demand for the product.

Some of the most popular brand of drone product in the market today in Nigeria is Gidi Drone Ltd among others. These very popular products should be benchmarked when strategizing on sales plan.

It is also added advantage if a unique mould is designed for the product. This gives the product an image and an impression of quality.

QUALITY CONTROL

Drone products are manufactured internationally with materials like to pose risk to human health in Nigeria, perhaps, during use or after disposure. This why the standards and requirements mapped out by Standard Organization of Nigeria, Nigeria Industrial System and among others must be fully complied with.

The following document needs to be obtained as a certification that the product is safe for the human environment.

(A) Product certificate (PC) Issued by Cotecna

(b) Certificate of Conformity (CoC), which is well known as SONCAP Certificate (SC), Issued by Cotecnac

There are also other important requirements such as certificate of analysis of the product to be obtained from a public analyst and Standard Operational Procedure (SOP).

CHAPTER FOUR

CAPITAL EXPENDITURE

ACCOMMODATION

However, in order to successfully operate the business, there is need to provide a good accommodation in form of warehouse for product storage as well as retail stores outlets for sells and customer interaction. With the warehouse, extra products and parts safety can be assured and well stored for easy retrival on sale demand. The store here can be referred to as an office. Too, it all depends on, which works best for you. A good and wide warehouse and stores are highly needed and therefore the sum of N250, 000 will be budgeted for the securing and face lift of the buildings. The money will take care of the landlord or agent settlement, house rent and repairs. The location of the accommodation must be on highly commercial area in Lagos state; Ikoyi, Victoria and Lagos Island, Lekki e.t.c should be major target due to the purchasing power in those areas of Lagos state

UTILITIES (GENERATOR SET)

The poor nature of electricity power supply implies maintaining a standby generator as to ensure steady power supply and testing of the product for potential buyers. There is need for a customer to experience lights, fresh air and comfort as he or she walks into the store.

The cost is set at N150,000 in order to purchase a heavy load carrier and quality generator.

MOTOR VEHICLE

There is need to provide a working vehicle for the project, which will play a great role in the evacuation and distribution of finished products and parts materials all around Lagos. That will save more cost compared to when paid transport are used for the activity.

One panel van will be provided for it. The sum of N750, 000 will be earmarked for it.

Based on the above, the total projected cost for the capital expenses is stated as follows

Accommodation	N250,000
Utilities (Generator set)	N150,000

Motor vehicle	N750,000
Fixtures and fittings	N200,000
Total	**N1,350,000**

FIXTURES AND FITTINGS

There will be need to procure some office equipments, fixtures and fittings. For, which the sum of 200,000 will be required for its accomplishment. This will help put a finishing touch to the building interior design and beauty to the test of the visitors.

Assets Depreciation Table

Year	1	2	3
Accommodation (5%)	79	79	79
Utilities (Generator set)	40	40	40

(20%)			
Motor Vehicles (20%)	200	200	200
Furniture and fittings (15%)	56	56	56
Total Depreciation	375	375	375
Cumulative Depreciation	375	750	1, 125

CHAPTER FIVE

OPERATIONAL EXPENSES

HUMAN RESOURCES REQUIREMENT

With regards to the business, the following staff will be required for a takeoff.

A.   Manager (One in number)

B. Sales/Account officer (One in number)

C. Engineer (One in number)

D. Marketing Officers (two in number)

E. Driver (One in number)

The academic requirement and cost implication of hiring their services are stated below:-

Status	Registered Number	Qualification	Monthly Salary/Allowances	Annual Salary	Total
Manager	1	B.Sc/HND Business Administration with minimum of 3 years	N35,000	420,000	420,000

		experience			
Engineer	1	HND Engineer with minimum of 3years experience	N35,000	420,000	420,000
Marketing Officers	2	OND with Minimum of 2years experience	N25,000	300,000	300,000
Sales/Acco unt officer	1	OND Business Administratio n/account with 2 years experience	N25,000	300,000	300,000
Driver	1	Driving license with minimum 2 years driving experience	N25,000	300,000	300,000

		Total	145,0 00	1,740,0 00	1,740,0 00

OTHER OPERATIONAL EXPENSES

UTILITIES

There should be cost of running the generator set and the vehicles.

The cost of fuel and oil for running the generator set and project vehicles is put at an estimated average cost of 1,000 per day (N1,000 x 250 working days). The total cost of N250, 000 is projected for this.

REPAIRS AND MAINTENANCE

The cost of repairs and maintenance is put at N150, 000 per year.

PROMOTION

There should be advertizement programme to promote the product for the purpose of awareness creation to the consumers.

The sum of N200, 000 would be earmarked in the first year to advertize on televisions, newspapers, print posters and handbills as well as website.

PRELIMINARY EXPENSES

There should be commitments to be made to standard Organization of Nigeria, Nigeria Industrial System among others. This is with regards to obtaining necessary certificates. The sum of N200, 000 will be earmarked for this.

Summary of operational expenses in a year at full capacity

Human resources cost   N1, 740,000

Other Operational expenses

Utilities
N200, 000

Repairs and maintenance
N150, 000

Promotion
N200, 000

Preliminary expenses
N200, 000

Total
N2, 490,000

CAPACITY UTILIZATION

Due to financial constraints, problems in penetration of the market as a new product and other unforeseen circumstances, the promoters may not be able to achieve full capacity sales coverage.

As a result, 50 percent capacity will be targeted in the first year, which will be subjected to 10 percent increase in subsequent years.

CHAPTER SIX

FINANCIAL PROJECTION

PROJECTED TAKE OFF PROJECT COST

Based on the cost evaluation carried out the project can be started with the estimated sum of **N1, 890, 000** as stated below:-

Capital investment
N1, 350,000

Human resources capital (1 month)
N145, 000

Other Operational expenses (6 months)

Utilities

N125, 000

Repairs and maintenance

N75, 000

Promotion

N100, 000

Preliminary expenses

N50, 000

Total

N1, 890, 000

The working capital provision is made only for one month.

Other operational expenses including SON/NIS and legal requirements and other associated operational expenses and provision are estimated for six months.

REVENUE PROJECTION

Due to the uniqueness of the scientific technology and non vital competition, the price is saleable. Just as it was during the rise of telecommunication in Nigeria, where a mobile phone worth 10,000 now was sold at 100,000, which was due to its uniqueness and lack of competition which is normalized today because of active competition. Let's assume the product is priced at the rate of 300,000 naira and two is being sold every blessed day. Research findings shows Gidi drone Ltd, Online shops like Jumia and Konga sells not less than four each day. We choose two in order not to make unforeseeable prediction. This will be a new brand company and product but the marketing and advertizing strategies will scale it through. What really matters in a new product is advertisement and marketing. Profit projections being carried out here does not cover the sales and profits to be made from selling of its parts like cameras and repairs for, which lots of money can be made from it.

Going by the above projection

In a day

In a day the products mapped out for sale is 2

In a month (21 days)

In a month the products mapped out for sale is 2 x 21 = 42

In a year (250 working days)

In a year the products mapped out for sale is 2 x 250 = 500

Current market price of drone product

Based on market survey, drone product is sold at the rate of 350,000. Though, it comes in categories. But we will be are price at 300,000, which implies that:

In a day

2 products will be sold which is 2 x 300,000 = 600,000

In a month (21 days)

2 products will be sold which is 42 x 300,000 = 12,600,000

In a year (250 working days)

2 products will be sold which is 500 x 300, 000 = 150,000,000

GROSS PROFIT (1ST YEAR)

Projected revenue/turnover	N150, 000,000
Capital/operational expenses	N3, 850,000
Gross profit	**N1, 461,500**

From the turn over you can calculate your cost of product as to arrive to the net profit

PROJECTED PROFIT AND LOSS ACCOUNT

Year	1	2	3
Units of products			
	500	1,000	1,500
Selling price			
	N300,000	300,000	330,000

Projected Revenue			
Total (N'000)	**150,000**	**300,000**	**495,000**
Cost of expenses			
Capital investment	1, 350	1, 350	1, 350
Staff	145	125	125
Utilities	250	275	303
Repairs & maintenance	150	170	185
Promotion	200	220	242
Preliminary expenses	200		
Total expenses (N'000)	2,295	2,160	2,225
Gross profit (N'000)	147, 705	297, 840	492,775

PROJECTED CASH FLOW STATEMENT

Year	1	2	3
Cash inflow(N'000)			
Turnover/Revenue	**150,000**	**300,000**	**495,000**
Capital investment	1, 350	1, 350	1, 350
Staff	145	145	145
Utilities	250	275	303
Repairs & maintenance	150	170	185
Promotion	200	220	242
Preliminary expenses	200		
Total cash outflow	**2,295**	**2,160**	**2,225**
Total Cash surplus	**147,705**	**297,840**	**492,775**

REFERENCE

Textbooks
 Nwachukwu C. (2010). Management: theory & practice
Lagos; pacific publishers Ltd

Adekunle A. (2014). Nigerian economy challenges
Abuja; Spectrum books limited

Femi G. (2012). Five major principles of project
management
London; greenwood press

Umunna C. (2015) "Planning and budgeting"
Paper presentation. Nigeria forum, vol. 26. Page 5-6.

Okonkwo M. (2014). Nigerian market opportunities
Onitsha; Noben press Limited

Obikeze S. (2010). State of the nation: Nigeria
Lagos; Longman publishers

Achebe W. (2016). "How large is Nigerian market"
 Paper presentation. Entreprenuers conference

Online Resources
Sattler T. (2016) Drone Business Plan. Retrieved from
htt://www.business-plans.com/drone-business-plan/

Miranda. M. (2015, September 10th) The beginners guide
to starting a drone business. Retrieved from

http://blog.dronesetc.com/industries/the-beginners-guide-to-starting-a-drone-based-business/

Online directory (n.d). List of market researchers in Nigeria. Retrieved from http://www.businesslist.com.ng/category/market-reserch

SONCAP (2016). How do I get a certificate? Retrieved from http://www.exports2nigeria.com/how-do-i-get-a-certificate

Standard Organization of Nigeria official site http://son.gov.ng

Nigeria Galleria (2015). Market research. Retrieved from www.nigeriagalleria.com/business_services/marketing_research.html

Adewale (2016). Nigerians can now buy drones on gidi drone. Retrieved from http://techcityng.com/nigerians-can-now-buy-drones-on-gidi-drone/

World Population Review (2014). Population of Lagos state. Retrieved from http://worldpopulationreview.com/world-cities/lagos-population/